ABUNDANT TRUTH
            MINISTRIES

Potter's Wheel Study Series

The Forming of the Prophet

The Preparation of the Prophet and Prophetic Minister for Ministry and Service

Roderick Levi Evans

The Forming of the Prophet

The Preparation of the Prophet and Prophetic Minister for Ministry and Service

All Rights Reserved © 2024 by Roderick L. Evans

Front & Back Cover Designs by Abundant Truth
Image by riteshphotography from Pixabay

Abundant Truth Publishing
an imprint of Abundant Truth International Ministries

For information address:
Abundant Truth International
P.O. Box 126
Camden, NC 27921

Unless otherwise indicated all of the scripture quotations are taken from the Authorized King James Version of the Bible. Scripture quotations marked with NIV are taken from the New International Version of the Bible. Scriptures marked with NASV are taken for the New American Standard Version of the Bible.

978-1-60141-574-5

Printed in the United States of America

Contents

Introduction

Chapter 1- Crushing of the Prophet   1

The Potter's Decision   4

The Prophet's Predicament   5

Chapter 2 - Reverence of the Prophet   9

The Lord's Glory   11

The Prophet's Self-Awareness   13

Chapter 3 - Building of the Prophet   17

Spiritual Maturity   20

Motivation   21

Resolve   21

Authority   22

Contents (cont.)

Submission   23

Chapter 4 – The Prophet's Character (1)   **29**

The Foundation of Love   31

Chapter 5 – The Prophet's Character (2)   **41**

The Foundation of Love (continued)   43

Bibliography   **53**

Introduction

Ministry and service in the kingdom of God is a privilege. God calls every member of the Body of Christ to serve for the benefit and welfare of the Body of Christ. However, we must remember that there are personal preparations that God requires for service.

The Potter's Wheel Study Series is designed to help believers recognize and apply the personal preparation that God implements for those called to minister and to serve. It is our prayer that the minister and the laymen will respond to God's personal preparations for ministry and service.

In this Publication

The prophet's ministry comes with responsibility, authority, and power. In order for an individual to operate effectively in this ministry, his/her character has to be solid. Therefore, God will take the prophet through tests, trials, and temptations in order to prepare them for ministry.

The training of a prophet is sometimes painful. God will deal with every area in his life to prepare him for service. Those called to the prophetic office should understand that preparation for ministry is in character, not solely in the development of spiritual gifts. In this book, we will discuss how God builds the prophet and prophetic minister for ministry.

THE FORMING OF THE PROPHET

-Chapter 1-

Crushing of the Prophet:

The Potter's Wheel

THE FORMING OF THE PROPHET

POTTER'S WHEEL STUDY SERIES

THE FORMING OF THE PROPHET

Jeremiah prophesied to Judah during a time of great rebellion and sin against God. Prophetically, the Lord compared his dealing with Judah to a potter working on a wheel.

The word which came to Jeremiah from the Lord, saying, Arise, and go down to the potter's house, and there I will cause thee to hear my words. Then I went down to the potter's house, and, behold, he wrought a work on the wheels. And the vessel that he made of clay was marred in the hand of the potter: so he made it again another vessel, as seemed good to the

THE FORMING OF THE PROPHET

potter to make it. (Jeremiah 18:1-4)

The Potter's Decision

Jeremiah saw the potter making a vessel that seemed good in his eyes. God does this with the prophet. The prophet cannot decide what 'type' of prophet he will be. This is God's decision alone. His whole life becomes a prophetic example to the world.

Therefore, God will allow trials and sufferings as a part of the prophet's training and discipline. These are designed to produce humility in the prophet. God will build the prophet up only to break him down again so that the prophet knows that he is God's vessel and no longer his own.

The Prophet's Predicament

In Jeremiah's description of the potter, it was the potter who marred the vessel. Most prophets have stories of great affliction and pain. It seems that God will allow them to be forsaken, ostracized, misunderstood, experience health problems, and the like in order to break down the mentality of the prophet.

This is so God can build the prophet again into a vessel that will serve in holiness, power, and integrity.

THE FORMING OF THE PROPHET

Jeremiah saw the potter working on a solitary vessel. This implies that prophets will go through times of separation from their peers and other personalities as God makes them. God calls prophets to a greater level of self-death than others, so that His mind and heart will be communicated without personal biases or influences from the prophet.

In addition, God's training and crushing of the prophet continues throughout the life of the prophet to preserve him from personal sin and rebellion; that the word of the Lord from him will remain pure and untainted.

THE FORMING OF THE PROPHET

Notes:

THE FORMING OF THE PROPHET

THE FORMING OF THE PROPHET

-Chapter 2-

Reverence of the Prophet:

Isaiah's Vision

THE FORMING OF THE PROPHET

POTTER'S WHEEL STUDY SERIES

THE FORMING OF THE PROPHET

Isaiah's call to a greater prophetic ministry was inaugurated with the reception of a vision of the Lord. While in the Temple, God revealed His glory to him.

The Lord's Glory

Isaiah saw the Lord upon His throne and His glory filling the Temple. He beheld the seraphim who cried out because of the Lord's holiness. Upon seeing these things, Isaiah realized God's greatness and his own sinfulness.

> *Then said I, Woe is me! for I am undone; because I am a man of unclean lips, and I dwell in the midst of a people of unclean lips:*

THE FORMING OF THE PROPHET

for mine eyes have seen the King, the Lord of hosts. (Isaiah 6:5)

When God prepares the prophet for service, the prophet will be confronted with God's greatness. This is to produce in the prophet an unwavering reverence and fear for the Lord. In turn, the prophet will execute his ministry understanding the greatness of the One whom he represents.

Prophets will minister powerful messages from the Lord. Except the prophet respects God and understands his relationship to the Lord, the prophet will exalt his ministry above the God that called him.

THE FORMING OF THE PROPHET

The Prophet's Self-Awareness

When Isaiah saw God's glory, he realized his own sinfulness and that he could not glory in himself. The prophet today will experience a similar encounter with the Lord.

Without a proper reverence for the Lord, the prophet may become disobedient or mishandle the prophetic ministry.

Thus, God will reveal His glory so that the prophet may fear. Prophetic ministry produces fear and respect for the prophet. However, the prophet has to understand that God will not share His glory.

I am the Lord: that is my name:

THE FORMING OF THE PROPHET

and my glory will I not give to another, neither my praise to graven images. (Isaiah 42:8)

God reveals His glory so that the prophet will challenge the Body of Christ to reverence God. God uses men and women, but they are not to be equated with God, or be feared as God. God repeatedly declares His supremacy over men in the scriptures.

When God's process of developing reverence in the prophet is complete, the prophet will endeavor to turn the people's attention to God and not themselves as they minister.

THE FORMING OF THE PROPHET

Notes:

THE FORMING OF THE PROPHET

THE FORMING OF THE PROPHET

-Chapter 3-

Building of the Prophet:

Nebuchadnezzar's Dream

THE FORMING OF THE PROPHET

POTTER'S WHEEL STUDY SERIES

THE FORMING OF THE PROPHET

God develops humility and reverence in the prophet to build them into profitable servants. There are general characteristics that every prophet possesses as a result of the Lord's building process.

The image that Nebuchadnezzar saw gives a clear illustration of how God builds the prophet.

This image's head was of fine gold, his breast and his arms of silver, his belly and his thighs of brass, His legs of iron, his feet part of iron and part of clay.

Thou sawest till that a stone was cut out without hands, which smote the image upon his feet that were of iron and clay and brake them to pieces. (Daniel 2:32-34)

Spiritual Maturity

Head of Gold. The head of gold reflects the wisdom, knowledge, understanding, and revelation that God gives the prophet.

As gold is tried in the fire, so God will instruct, rebuke, and discipline the prophet in knowledge of His ways, statutes, and Word.

For thou preventest him with the blessings of goodness: thou settest a crown of pure gold on his head. (Psalms 21:3)

Motivation

Breast and Arms of Silver. The breast and arms of silver reflects the prophet's motivation for ministry. The breast (chest) is the place where the heart is, and the arms represent what the prophet will reach and strive for. Thus, as silver is purified, God builds the prophet to have proper motives in ministry.

For thou, O God, hast proved us: thou hast tried us, as silver is tried. (Psalm 66:10)

Resolve

Belly and Thighs of Brass. The belly and thighs of brass reflects the prophet's resolve and stamina in

THE FORMING OF THE PROPHET

ministry. The prophet has to have his fleshly desires under control (represented by the stomach) and walk upright before the Lord (represented by the thighs). The prophet is built to endure test and attacks, remaining faithful to the Lord and ministry.

> *Therefore, my beloved brethren, be ye stedfast, unmoveable, always abounding in the work of the Lord, forasmuch as ye know that your labour is not in vain in the Lord. (I Corinthians 15:58)*

Authority

Feet of Iron and Clay. The feet of iron and clay reflect the prophet's authority in ministry. The iron represents the strength and authority of the Word that he will carry.

The clay speaks of the prophet's humility while operating in great authority. The prophet must possess authority and humility as he performs his ministry.

> *For thou hast made him a little lower than the angels, and hast crowned him with glory and honour. Thou madest him to have dominion over the works of thy hands; thou hast put all things under his feet. (Psalms 8:5-6)*

Submission

Stone Made Without Hands. At

the end of the dream, a stone came and brake the image in pieces. We know that the stone was a representation of Christ. This reflects the prophet's submission to Christ in ministry. No matter how great God makes a prophet, he has to remember that if he exalts himself, God will bring him down.

And whosoever shall exalt himself shall be abased; and he that shall humble himself shall be exalted. (Matthew 23:12)

The greatness that a prophet has comes from God. The prophet has to walk in the knowledge that before Christ, his gifts, calling, and ministry mean nothing.

THE FORMING OF THE PROPHET

Whosoever shall fall upon that stone shall be broken; but on whomsoever it shall fall, it will grind him to powder. (Luke 20:18)

God crushes, produces reverence, and builds the prophet so that the prophet will have character conducive to facilitating pure and powerful prophetic ministry.

THE FORMING OF THE PROPHET

THE FORMING OF THE PROPHET

Notes:

THE FORMING OF THE PROPHET

-Chapter 4-

The Prophet's Character (1):

The Way of Love

THE FORMING OF THE PROPHET

THE FORMING OF THE PROPHET

Prophets speak for God, who is love. Regardless of the message delivered, the prophet's motivation for ministry has to be love. Love should be the foundation for the prophet's character. Love brings balance to the prophets as they deliver messages of rebuke and correction.

The Foundation of Love

I Corinthians 13 gives us a list of the attributes of love. Fifteen traits are listed. Wherever the word "love" is, replace it with "a prophet." If prophets speak the heart of God, the heart of God must be in them.

Love is patient; love is kind. It does not envy; it does not boast;

it is not proud. It is not rude; it is not self-seeking; it is not easily angered; it keeps no record of wrongs. Love does not delight in evil but rejoices with the truth. It always protects, always trusts, always hopes, always perseveres. Love never fails. (I Corinthians 13:4-8a NASV)

Patient. Prophets have to be patient. Patience has to govern them as they wait to see the Church act on what God reveals to them. The prophet has the responsibility to deliver the word. The hearer has the task of carrying it out.

THE FORMING OF THE PROPHET

Prophets have to be patient with pastors and others as they follow the word spoken by them. The prophet may not know the timing that God has for a particular word.

> *And the servant of the Lord must not strive; but be gentle unto all men, apt to teach, patient. (II Timothy 2:24)*

Kind. Prophets have to be nice people. Because they sometimes will speak rebuke and correction, it is no excuse for them to be overbearing and rude. They have to behave as recipients of the grace and compassion of God.

THE FORMING OF THE PROPHET

Not envious. Prophets must resist the desire to compete. They should not be envious of another's ministry or position. Envy opens up the prophet to demonic influence in his life. James states that envy leads to evil.

> *For where envying and strife is, there is confusion and every evil work. (James 3:16)*

Envying causes prophets to covet power and position. They will, in turn, prophesy from their own opinions and thoughts. This enables a stronghold of the enemy in their lives.

Not boastful. Prophets hear from God frequently. They have to guard themselves against bragging about their relationship with God. God's call to ministry is a call to humility.

Prophets must not use their gifts as a vehicle for promotion or honor. The true road to honor comes from obedience and submission to God.

Humble yourselves in the sight of the Lord, and he shall lift you up. (James 4:10)

Not proud. Prophets must resist pride at all costs. God gives them great authority in the Spirit realm. However, they should not confuse

THE FORMING OF THE PROPHET

their spiritual authority with self-worth. The call to ministry is not a platform for self-exaltation.

> *But he giveth more grace. Wherefore he saith, God resisteth the proud, but giveth grace unto the humble. (James 4:6)*

Any prophet who operates in pride will not have a fruitful ministry. God's dealing with him will be infrequent and miniscule. Prophets should remember that God resists the proud.

Not rude. Prophets have to be courteous in their actions. Ministry is not an excuse for rude behavior. Some prophets blame their harsh statements and gestures on the Spirit. Though rebuke and correction do not feel or sound nice, it must be delivered out of a pure spirit.

Because prophets face rejection regularly, some are vulnerable to expressing their bitterness and hurt through ministry. Prophets are to avoid this at all costs.

Not self-seeking. Prophets must not regard or use their ministries as platforms for personal gain. They prophesy out of obedience to God, not man. Any self-seeking prophet walks in the way of Balaam, the false prophet, whom Balak asked to curse Israel.

THE FORMING OF THE PROPHET

Prophets that are self-seeking will become false prophets and share the same fate as he did. God rebuked him and later killed him.

> *Which have forsaken the right way, and are gone astray, following the way of Balaam the son of Bosor, who loved the wages of unrighteousness; But was rebuked for his iniquity: the dumb ass speaking with man's voice forbad the madness of the prophet. (II 2:15-16)*

Not easily angered. Prophets become vulnerable to anger when they are ignored. Prophets have to remember, they represent God. If people do not listen to them, it is not grounds for

THE FORMING OF THE PROPHET

them to become angry. Prophets speak for God and not themselves.

For the wrath of man worketh not the righteousness of God. (James 1:20)

Though prophets speak with the mind and wisdom of God, their anger does not always reflect this. Prophets who have tempers should remember the examples of Moses and Jonah.

Moses, for his outburst of anger, was not allowed to enter into Canaan; while Jonah endured a harsh lesson from the Lord.

THE FORMING OF THE PROPHET

THE FORMING OF THE PROPHET

Notes:

THE FORMING OF THE PROPHET

THE FORMING OF THE PROPHET

-Chapter 5-

The Prophet's Character (2):

The Way of Love

THE FORMING OF THE PROPHET

THE FORMING OF THE PROPHET

In this chapter, we continue our discussion of the prophet's character founded upon love.

The Foundation of Love (continued)

Keeps no record of wrong. In personal and ministerial life, the prophet has to learn to forgive. Forgiveness is the duty of all believers. Prophets have to be forgiving when they are misunderstood.

> *And be ye kind one to another, tenderhearted, forgiving one another, even as God for Christ's sake hath forgiven you. (Ephesians 4:32)*

Prophets, also, have to release individuals whom God forgives.

THE FORMING OF THE PROPHET

Prophets see the sins and faults of others. They must learn to release individuals from past sins and not judge. In addition, prophets are not to share revealed sins to other believers.

Does not rejoice in evil. Prophets have to guard their hearts against being happy when individuals experience the discipline of God.

Jonah hoped for the destruction of Nineveh; he was angered when God had mercy.

Prophets have to remember that God's discipline comes because of His love. In addition, prophets must remember that God delights in mercy.

> *But go ye and learn what that meaneth, I will have mercy, and not sacrifice: for I am not come to call the righteous, but sinners to repentance. (Matthew 9:13)*

> *For he saith to Moses, I will have mercy on whom I will have mercy, and I will have compassion on whom I will have compassion. (Romans 9:15)*

Rejoices with the truth. Contrary to popular belief, prophets are not to be sad individuals. They should be able to rejoice with the truth, even in adverse settings.

THE FORMING OF THE PROPHET

For which cause we faint not; but though our outward man perish, yet the inward man is renewed day by day. (II Corinthians 4:16)

Though some truth they carry may be unpopular, prophets have to learn to keep their spirits refreshed and renewed, even in persecution.

Protects. Prophets serve as protectors of the Word of God and the Church. Prophets will guard the Church against false doctrines and spiritual deception.

In addition, they will help leadership protect immature and

weak Christians. They will also aid in their restoration after a fall.

> *We then that are strong ought to bear the infirmities of the weak, and not to please ourselves. (Romans 15:1)*

Always trusts. Prophets not only have to trust God, but also fellow believers. Prophets have to resist becoming judgmental of others, using "discernment" as an excuse.

False discernment develops out of a bruised and hurt spirit. Prophets have to keep personal feelings aside in ministry. They need to learn to stay in the Spirit when discerning.

THE FORMING OF THE PROPHET

Hopes. Prophets are to live by faith and be able to inspire faith in others.

Prophets are faced with adverse situations from the Church, family, and the enemy. Except hope remains, the prophet will become subject to disappointment and discouragement. This is what happened to Jeremiah. He asked,

> *Why is my pain perpetual, and my wound incurable, which refuseth to be healed? Wilt thou be altogether unto me as a liar, and as waters that fail? (Jeremiah 15:18)*

Jeremiah had lost hope because his ministry met great opposition. A true

THE FORMING OF THE PROPHET

prophet's ministry is always under scrutiny and judgment. Without hope, the prophet will become burnt-out and disillusioned.

Perseveres. Prophets need endurance. They have to persevere through the tests of God, temptations of the devil, trials of men, and the troubles of life. Without perseverance, prophets will give up during hard times. In addition, their lives and ministries will be short-lived.

The gifts and callings of God are without repentance, but the nature of God has to be developed. Because of the spiritual depth of their ministries, prophets need depth of character for balance. Prophets will not fail in their

THE FORMING OF THE PROPHET

ministries as long as they walk in love.

For a full examination of the prophetic ministry, see my book, "If They Be Prophets: An Examination of the Prophetic Office and Gift."

THE FORMING OF THE PROPHET

Notes:

THE FORMING OF THE PROPHET

THE FORMING OF THE PROPHET

Evans, Roderick L. (2012). If They Be Prophets: An Examination of the Prophetic Office and Gift. Abundant Truth Publishing. Camden, NC, 2012

Lockman Foundation. *Comparative Study Bible.* Zondervan Publishing House. Grand Rapids, MI, c1984

Merriam-Webster Online Dictionary Copyright © 2005 by Merriam-Webster, Incorporated. All rights reserved.

The Bible Library. *The Bible Library CD Rom Disc.* Ellis Enterprises Incorporated, (c)

THE FORMING OF THE PROPHET

1988 – 2000. 4205 McAuley Blvd., Suite 385, Oklahoma City, OK 73120. All Rights Reserved.

THE FORMING OF THE PROPHET

Notes:

THE FORMING OF THE PROPHET

THE FORMING OF THE PROPHET

Notes:

THE FORMING OF THE PROPHET

THE FORMING OF THE PROPHET

Notes:

THE FORMING OF THE PROPHET

THE FORMING OF THE PROPHET

Notes:

THE FORMING OF THE PROPHET

THE FORMING OF THE PROPHET

Notes:

THE FORMING OF THE PROPHET

THE FORMING OF THE PROPHET

Notes:

THE FORMING OF THE PROPHET

THE FORMING OF THE PROPHET

Notes:

THE FORMING OF THE PROPHET

Made in United States
Orlando, FL
16 September 2024